The Secret of the Sabbath

Understanding the Lord's Day... and Living It

Richard M. Eyre

Ink Inc.
PUBLISHERS

Library of Congress Catalog Card Number: 79-52229
ISBN.1-555-17-179-6

We spend much time and money on self-help ideas, courses and books. But the best self-help idea, and the simplest, is proper observance of the Sabbath day, which can simplify our lives and cause the other six days and the other nine commandments to work together for our good.

Prologue

In the movie (and the true story) *Chariots of Fire*, the great Scottish runner Eric Liddle stands before the King of England and says *no* to the demand that he run an olympic race on Sunday. I love my country and serve my King, says Liddle, but there is a higher law, a higher obligation.

Liddle could well have said a higher *privilege*, a higher *promise*, because the Sabbath Day, when lived in compliance with scriptural admonition, provides *enormous* blessings and advantages.

The most simple and accurate way to perceive the true concept of *sabbatical* can be stated in one word: RENEWAL. Humans, like the soil of the earth they live upon, need regular rest, renewal, regeneration. Our minds and our spirits need it as much as our bodies.

Sleeping at night isn't enough. Taking a vacation once a year isn't enough. Meditation or planning periodically (or even once a day) isn't enough. Human beings are programmed, designed, engineered in such a way that we need a particular kind of revitalizing *rest* once each week. The rest we need is not just reduced activity—it is a *change* or orientation, a new perspective where instead of self-advancement, self-entertainment, or self-indulgence we shift paradigms and think longer-range from the standpoint of who we are eternally, who we are in relation to God, the state of our spirits, the state of our souls.

"Man was not made for the Sabbath but the Sabbath for man." One interpretation of these scriptural words is that the Sabbath was made for us and given to us that we might regularly rest, renew, rejuvenate and re-create

ourselves, our families and even our personalities and our characters.

This is not a book about the Sabbath Day as much as it is a book about "becoming" and improving within ourselves and our families, about living a fuller, happier life, about deepening our spirituality and our relationship with God . . . and about *using the Sabbath Day to bring these things about.*

This is a spiritual book more than a dogmatically religious one. It is spiritual by definition because it deals with our spirits—with our inner selves, with the attitudes of our minds and our hearts.

There are no required beliefs for readers of this book, but some of what it has to say will make more sense to you if you know some of the things *I* believe. It will make still more sense to you if you believe some or all of the same things.

1. I believe in a God who is personally interested in us, his children, and I believe in angels and in miracles (defined as things that happen by higher laws than those we know).
2. I believe that each of us has a spirit within us that is older than our bodies and that came from God. I believe that life continues after death, as do our opportunities to progress and to know God.
3. I believe that mortality—this earth, this life, with all of its options, opportunities and opposites—is a gift from God, designed to give us opportunities to progress and become more like Him. Families and relationships are the most important part of this development. We are fortunate to live near the close of this millennium when spiritual awareness is heightened and many spiritual truths are restored.

4. I believe in the Holy Bible and other scripture, and view all of the scriptural commandments not as arbitrary restrictions but as loving counsel from a wise Father who wants us to find joy.

5. I believe that Jesus Christ is the literal Son of God, our older spiritual brother, and the Savior and Redeemer of the world. Worshipping on Sunday and partaking of the Sacrament of the Lord's supper* is a useful way to focus on Him and re-commit ourselves to Him.

You will not be peculiar if you find yourself in substantial agreement on several of these beliefs. Recent polls relative to number one, for example, tell us that 98 percent of Americans believe in God and 78 percent believe in angels. Most Christians believe most of the above list, although there are parts of 2, 3, and 5 that are not official doctrines of most denominations.**

Sometimes, when we let ourselves believe, we find new levels of meaning. There will be some who discover, as they read both sides of this book, that they believe more than they thought they did.

RICHARD M. EYRE
WASHINGTON, D.C.—1995

* Often referred to in this book simply as "sacrament."

** For further clarification of these and other personal beliefs of the author, write to him directly c/o The Fischer Ross Group, Inc., 211 East 49th Street, New York City, NY, 10017.

Contents

Chapter 1

The Promises and the Key

All of God's commandments carry with them the promise of rewards.

But there is one particular commandment, the living of which is an art, that can bring these promises to fulfillment in your life:

— Regular access to God's guidance.
— A simpler, clearer view of life and of your purpose in life.
— Greater control over your own destiny.
— A happier, more unified family.
— An ability to better live all other commandments.
— A well-rested sense of well-being.
— Access to the good things of the earth (prosperity).
— A pattern of order and purpose in your life.
— Insight to your own potential.

— A deeper testimony and witness of Christ.
— A spiritual link to your ancestors and to your children.
— Inner peace in this world.
— Better relationships with family and friends.
— A marriage of true partnership and oneness.
— Eternal life in the world to come.

Sound like a wish list?

In a sense, it is. Everyone with hope and faith wishes for these gifts. They are the great promises, the great rewards of life, the products of God's plan for us.

And the key that unlocks the door to all of these promises is the full and creative living of one of God's commandments.

The key is the Sabbath day.

Keeping the Sabbath is far more than going to church and avoiding temporal work. It is a skill and an art that can actually make the other nine commandments easier.

Living every seventh day as God intends means far more than resting. It means re-creating in a way that makes the other six days full and fair and meaningful.

In the commandment of the Sabbath day (see Exodus 20:8-11; 23:12), the Lord gives us access to a great law of creativity and rejuvenation from which he wishes us to benefit. Man was not made for the Sabbath, but the Sabbath was made for man. (See Mark 2:27.) Indeed, it is God's gift for our use.

But how is it to be used? Just how does the law work? What is entailed in the art of correctly living the Sabbath day? And how can a day that is, for many of us, the most hectic and least restful, be turned into a day that is refreshing and renewing and that gives us the promises just listed?

Let's think about it together.

Chapter 2

The Law

A. The Lord's Day

The Lord calls the Sabbath his day. And yet, he tells us that the Sabbath was made for us. Is it his day or ours? Did he make it for us? Or did he make it for us to observe?

The answer is *both.*

He made the Sabbath for us to use for him. He made it for us to think of him and to begin to think like him. It is his day in that all we do should relate to him. It is his gift to us in that its proper use can give us clear insights into who he is and who we are to him.

It is his day given to us
> that we might strengthen our spirits,
> that we might renew our repentance,

that we might plan within his priorities and find our potential.

We cannot live the commandment and reap its promises when we forget that it is his day. If we use it to

seek our own pleasure or comfort,
speak our own words and ideas,
even set our own goals,
plan our own plans,

then we misuse his day and forfeit its promise.

But if we

seek his pleasure,
speak his words,
strive to learn his goals, his plans, and his foreordination for us,

then we use this gift as he intended; we unwrap his gift and it begins to work in our lives.

Remembering and observing the Lord's day honors the Lord, gives him all credit, and acknowledges his hand in all things.

B. *The First Day*

My grandfather was a master carpenter. As a boy I spent hours in his workshop. I remember the hum of the band saw, the curling shavings from the lathe, the smell of rough-cut cedar. And I remember one day trying to cut a board with a dull saw. There was a lot of action and a lot of heat but not much progress. Then grandfather took a file and sharpened the saw. After that, everything was better. My sawing sounded better, the smell in the room was like fresh sawdust instead of burning wood, and the saw sliced through the board like a loaf of bread.

How we slice our lives, how our lives feel, and what we accomplish is largely determined by how well and how often we sharpen our saw. Clear goals and plans, carefully, prayerfully, and regularly conceived, turn the contentions of confusion and chaos into the patterns of productivity and peace.

Because the Sabbath is the first day, it suggests forward vision and planning for the other six. The commandment to keep the Sabbath day is one of two among the Ten Commandments that is stated positively — what to do rather than what not to do.

This positive commandment about the first day suggests not a passive, dormant kind of rest but a living, recreating kind, like a basketball game's time-out . . . a reassessment, a redirection, a time to think about the action ahead and to determine the best course to take.

If we call a time-out every Sunday, a time-out from the race and selfishness of life, and if we use the time-out to seek perfect guidance from our Perfect Coach, then Sundays can become the window or opening through which light and energy flow, thus clearing

our vision, collecting our thoughts, calming our hearts.

Sundays can be the time when we conceive and plan the week ahead, when we create things spiritually before they occur physically. God created all things spiritually before they were naturally upon the earth. We can follow his example. We can use his gift of Sundays to spiritually create the physical, mental, emotional, and social facets of our lives, to figuratively, with his help, "write our diaries in advance," to begin each week with the end of the week in mind, and to act rather than react to life.

In the process, we must remember that we are always, but particularly on his day, looking not for our own goals but for his goals for us. The difference between planning for our own desires and gratification and planning for his will and purposes is the difference between seeking our self-given ambitions and seeking our God-given foreordinations.

Critics of personal goal-setting and planning say they can make us too structured, rigid, and self-centered. On the contrary. A person who uses a part of his Sunday to reassess, to think ahead, to seek guidance, and to plan resolves the problems that would otherwise occupy him and *frees* his mind to notice his surroundings, to recognize opportunities, to be more spontaneous, and to be more aware of other people and their needs. If our goals are prayerfully set, we become decreasingly self-centered and increasingly salvation-centered.

C. The Earth's Day

Cultivated land rejuvenates itself when it is given a sabbatical year, but it is more than that. Somehow the earth and the Sabbath are very closely and very naturally linked. Some of the blessings promised for proper Sabbath observance have to do with the fullness of the earth, the "good things" of the earth.

While we may not fully comprehend these connections, we can understand that the Sabbath is an eminently *natural* law, with natural consequences. Those who live it, who worship, rest, plan, and recreate will prosper. They will receive the earth's fullness and will be free and unspotted from the world's influences and less likely to contribute to the earth's malfunctions.

Prosperity and the "good things" of the earth are the downfall of many. But not of those who receive them through proper observance of the Sabbath, because this observance involves the humility of thinking of all things as belonging to God and of seeking his guidance in their use.

The core and essence of the law of the Sabbath is rejuvenation. God's intention is that we use the day

— to renourish our spirits,
— to recleanse our souls through repentance and confession,
— to recreate our inner selves and our outer directions,
— to recall the Lord's life and death and our baptismal commitments to him,
— to recharge our spiritual batteries,
— to renew our pursuit of potential, and

— to recommit ourselves to the working out of our own salvation.

Thought of in these terms, the keeping of the Sabbath is a law that lightens all other laws and a day that deepens all other days.

Chapter 3

The Objectives

As the last chapter concluded, the purpose of the Sabbath is rejuvenation and renewal of ourselves and of our commitments. The question of this chapter and the next two is how this purpose can translate into objectives and in turn into meaningful thoughts and actions on each Sabbath day.

Early in our marriage, Linda and I began to ask this question: What brings about rejuvenation and renewal?

The first and most obvious answer, it seemed, was worship and the thoughtful partaking of the sacrament. Here, baptism covenants are renewed along with loyalty and allegiance to Christ. Through worship and the sacrament we give ourselves to him so that he can renew us.

But just as faith is dead without works, we knew that trust in his renewing spirit without any effort on our part would produce little effect.

So we asked ourselves a more personal question: What can we do about our own renewal? What things do we have both the responsibility and the power to change? We decided that there were two basic things — ourselves and our family.

Renewal, then, spiritual rejuvenation and change, comes through three channels: (1) worship; (2) what we are becoming within ourselves; and (3) what we are becoming within our families. Together they draw on both faith and works, on our own efforts and on God's help, on effort and on grace. And together they make each Sunday another step on an eternally ascending staircase.

A. *Worship*

Worship is not something that church can do for us, or that partaking of the sacrament can bring about in us. Worship is a deeply personal and spiritual activity that we must practice and feel within ourselves. The scriptural instructions for sabbath observance include the offering of sacraments, the paying of devotions, the confession of sins, the acknowledgment of his hand, the renewing of fasting and thanksgiving—in short, the true loving of Christ and of the Father.

True worship is not something we can do on the spur of the moment. It requires preparation and a deeply sincere attitude. We should go to church hungering for the spiritual nourishment that can come from the sacrament and from our own humble devotion and covenant renewal.

The sacrament time itself should be one of reaching recommitment and increasing insight into the Spirit and person of Christ. We come to know people one facet or aspect at a time. By thinking and reading about one particular trait or quality of Christ before church each week, and thinking about that quality as we partake of his sacrament, we can know him better and can worship more intelligently. This pattern, of focusing on one aspect of Christ's character each week, is the subject of the other book in this volume.

An absolutely crucial part of true worship is repentance. Too often we think of repentance as a painful agony to be undertaken only in the aftermath of deep and mortal sin. In reality, repentance, the second principle of the gospel, is constantly needed for sins of all levels. None of us has ever lived even one perfect day, so all need to exhibit a repentant spirit all the time. And a repentance resolution to improve and grow should be a regular part of Sunday worship and the partaking of the sacrament.

The best measurement to determine what activities are appropriate on the Sabbath is the simple question, "Does it assist me to worship the Lord?"

A final thought on the objective of worship: As children of God, we are brothers and sisters of Jesus Christ. This doctrine does not lessen God, it lifts man. But we must be careful. We must not let our "closely related familiarity" with Christ lessen our awe for him. We must recognize that the difference between us is the difference between perfection and imperfection, between "everythingness" and "nothingness." As we come to know him, we will feel closer to him in terms of our communications, but further from him in terms of his perfection and our imperfection. In the words of Neal A. Maxwell, "The more we contemplate where we stand in relation to Christ the more we realize that we do not stand at all, we kneel." And in the words of C. S. Lewis, "Beware of professed Christians who possess insufficient *awe* of Christ.

B. *What We Are "Becoming" Within Ourselves*

A friend of mine once had two dreams about the Savior during the same night. I'm not certain that they were dreams of inspiration, but they were certainly dreams of insight.

In the first, she found herself seated on the Mount of Olives, listening to the Lord. The feeling she had was one of fear. She desperately hoped he would not look at her. She felt that she could not bear his direct gaze, that if his eyes were to look directly into hers they would see too much. Then he looked at her. And her feeling, stronger than any she had ever felt, was one of encircling love and the hope that he would never look away.

In her other dream she had died and was standing alone in a stark, beautiful white room, waiting for him. She had with her no belongings, no diplomas, no credentials, no friends, no letters of recommendation, no news clippings, no beautiful clothes or make-up. She was just there by herself. Her feeling was the simple realization that when we stand before God we are only who we really are.

While presiding over a mission in London, I often had occasion to ask missionaries and members in interviews and non-members in conversation what their most important objectives were. I got a lot of good answers and a lot not so good. They ranged from the memorization of scripture to the accumulation of wealth. I gradually realized that the problem with most goals is that they are external — they have to do with changing someone or something other than oneself.

The purpose of mortality is to work out our own salvation. The purpose of the Sabbath is to assist us

in this "working out." It is when we significantly change ourselves for the better that we are of great use to others, to the world, and to God.

A key objective of the Sabbath day should be the reevaluation of who we really are on the inside and of who we are becoming.

And this goal is not separate from the first objective outlined in this chapter, for the finest and longest-range method of worshiping the Lord is to take steps to become more like him.

C. What We Are "Becoming" Within Our Families

Many Christians believe that marriage and family relationships endure beyond death. In that paradigm, mortality is the beginning point for eternal families that are part of God's larger family. Regardless of religious belief, most people recognize the preeminent importance and priority of family.

Sundays should be regular and effective points of review and realignment concerning what our families are becoming.

It may be long after this earth that our families become true kingdoms, but they can become, here and now, true institutions.

An institution, in the most positive sense of the word, is a body with laws, standards, and traditions —a body that offers its members not only security and a sense of belonging but also growth, challenge, and assistance in mutual progression.

Our families should be great institutions, safe and secure ports from the storms and tempests of the world.

Making a family an institution is hard work and requires parental dedication and ideas and procedures like those outlined in the next chapter. It also requires keeping of the Sabbath day, the day when we take time to look at what we are becoming, to redirect our course and reset our sails.

The objectives of the Sabbath are (1) worship; (2) becoming what we should be within ourselves; and (3) becoming what we should be within our families. It is crucial that we balance these three objectives. Someone who puts all his focus on objective 1 may spend his whole Sunday in church at the neglect of

his family. Someone wholly oriented to objective 2 may become self-centered. Someone aiming only at objective 3 will perhaps spend all of his Sunday time on family at-home activities. But when the three objectives are balanced they assist each other and make the Sabbath a day of joy.

Knowing what we should do on the Sabbath is usually easier than doing it. The goals are easier than the plans. The *what* is easier than the *how*. The long-range theory is easier than the day-to-day method. The next chapter will discuss methods of working out day-to-day details.

Chapter 4

The Methods

The theoretical and conceptual portion of this book is now over. Hopefully the reader is now convinced that the Sabbath can be the great simplifier and orchestrator of life, and that its objectives should be the worship of God and the full "becoming" of self and of family.

This chapter is a list. A list of suggested methods. A list of ideas that might be applied in your family. A list of possible ways to approach the three objectives. Some potentially apply to everyone, some to families with younger children, and some to families with older children. For the most part they are ideas we or friends of ours have tried with success in our own families, but none of them represents "official" counsel. Not all of the ideas will appeal to you, and none of the ideas may be as good for you as the ideas you may gain yourself. But these pages will trigger your thoughts, renew your re-

solve, clarify your course. So select only the ideas that appeal to you most. Add to them your own approaches, and design a Sabbath program that is realistic to you and that maximizes your own personal and family observance of the Lord's day.

We will deal with the suggested methods under the same headings as the objectives that were discussed in the previous chapter. First some ways to improve worship, then ideas for internal "becoming," then suggestions for family "becoming."

A. *For Worship*

1. *Set the Sabbath mood.* Most of us, and particularly our children, need more than the word *Sunday* on the top of our calendars to impress upon us the uniqueness and specialness of the Lord's day. It helps to find particular ways to differentiate the Sabbath from other days — to start it differently, to approach it respectfully, to set an appropriate mood as it begins. Setting a Sabbath mood is like tuning in to the frequency of the Spirit. As we tune the mood to a pattern of peace and calmness, the spirit transmits its message and joy to us in ever-clearer channels.

   a. *Music.* Most of us have certain favorite classical or sacred music selections that lift us and calm us. And most of us could find more music that affects us in this way. Select records on Saturday night and turn them on first thing Sunday morning.

   b. *Poetry.* Like music, good poetry can have a calming, refining effect. Beautiful verse, read silently or aloud, either to oneself or to one's family, can invite a peaceful spirit.

   c. *Whispering.* Start the day softly. Let the music remind you to move a little slower, to think and act in a more thoughtful, peaceful way. Families will find that whispering is contagious. Even small children will do it when everyone else does. It will attract the Spirit and add to the distinctiveness of Sunday.

   d. *The visual mood.* Several years ago, we noticed that there was a very warm and special spirit in our home at Christmastime. It seemed

to us that the spirit of giving, of anticipation and excitement, of warmth and of family love, and most importantly the spirit of Christ at Christmastime, was very much the same spirit that we wanted in our home on Sunday — every Sunday.

So we started putting up a little green artificial Christmas tree early each Sunday morning. For us, it symbolized the warmth of Christmas and reminded us of that day and of its spirit. It also became the visual trigger for the children to be calm and quiet, peaceful and loving. I hadn't realized just how well it was working until one Sunday morning when our most rambunctious child, age four, came war-whooping down the hall as he usually does, wheeled around the corner, saw the little tree, put his hand over his mouth and walked softly and slowly into the kitchen to kneel down for family prayer.

It doesn't have to be a Christmas tree, of course. A special picture of the Savior that is put up only on Sundays might work as well or better. But some mood-setting visual presence helps.

The Christmas comparison is an interesting one. Indeed, if we celebrate Christ's birth once a year, we should celebrate his resurrection fifty-two times a year — and that is what we do on a sacrament-partaking Sabbath.

e. *"Sunday only."* Particularly with small children, it is good to have certain special things that are used only on Sunday, things that

cause children to look forward to Sunday and that are worship-connected. These can be a favorite book about Jesus, a classical record or tape that they particularly like, or a religious game that the family plays.

f. *"Never on Sunday."* Just as you have some special things that you do only on Sunday, have some unspecial things that you do only on non-Sundays. On Sundays, don't shop, don't watch TV, don't read a newspaper.

This book is much more concerned with what to do than with what not to do on the Sabbath, and the theory is that if we are intent on using the Lord's day well, we will have no time to do things that do not build our individual souls and our individual families. But there are some factors, like television sets and Sunday newspapers, that are subtle intruders into the Sabbath spirit, and these should be pushed off the Sunday calendar and onto another day.

g. *"The best."* The "firstlings of the flock," "the fatted calf" — it is always our best that we give to the Lord. And so it should be with the Lord's day. Use your best china; wear your finest clothes all day, not just in church. Refine your whole atmosphere as a token of worship and respect.

2. *The sacrament.* We often talk about the importance of the sacrament. It is the purpose for sacrament meeting, it is the renewal of our covenants, and it is the pivotal moment of the Sabbath. But few of us make the sacrament service as meaningful or as fulfilling or as renewing as it could be.

It should be a time devoted to serious effort in coming to better know the Lord.

a. *"What Manner of Man."* In addition to the Atonement, think of one separate, new aspect of the Savior's personality or character each week during the sacrament. Perhaps it would be his compassion for the poor and sick, or his love for little children, or his physical endurance and strength. Determine what quality or characteristic you will think about before going to church. Use the other book in this volume as your guide. It is truly remarkable how much better you can feel you know the Lord after a year (fifty-two sacrament experiences) of thinking of a new aspect of him each week.

b. *Focusing children's attention.* Elementary age children are old enough to participate in the "What Manner of Man" approach outlined above, but younger children need a simpler method. Help your preschoolers make a special picture scrapbook into which they put their favorite pictures of Jesus. Let the children look at the pictures only during the sacrament. Talk to them beforehand about what they should think about as they look at Jesus and remember him during the sacrament.

As home videotapes become more available it is possible to further enhance this practice. Each week, immediately before going to church, we play a fifteen- or twenty-minute segment of the eight-hour film *Jesus of Nazareth* on the television for the children. The film

has a beautiful, calming quality no matter which segment of the Savior's life we watch. Then we take the book *Jesus of Nazareth* (pictures taken from the film) to church and let the younger children look through it quietly and reverently during the sacrament. Our children dearly love both the film and the book and know that they can see them only on Sunday.

c. *Family Sunday service.* Occasionally travel or vacations or other factors will cause an individual or family to be unable to attend church on a given Sunday. To hold a family service can be a meaningful and memorable experience. Take time to talk about the sacrament and its meaning and how much you will all appreciate it when next you can partake of it.

d. *Missing the sacrament.* We are taught that there are times when we should not partake. If there is something unresolved and unrepented, it is good for the soul to have to miss the sacrament. In this context we really do miss it; we long for it and hunger for it and become firmer in our repentance and resolve.

e. *Repentance.* The missing of the sacrament just mentioned should be infrequent. But there is never a Sunday when we do not need some measure of repentance. Prior to church, focus your thoughts on the past week and on any actions or thoughts that require repentance. Think of those things and ask for forgiveness during the sacrament. Resolve and commit not to repeat them. Write them later in a private place in your diary or date book. If

apologies to others or any form of restitution
are needed, plan and write down when you
will do so.

True freedom from sin, which we reach for as
an abiding joy, can be obtained and main-
tained only through consistent striving for
repentance.

3. *The scriptures.* While the scriptures should be
read every day, individuals and families should
have special scripture-based worship on Sundays.

    a. *Memorization.* Memorizing is a wonderful
        mental discipline for children as well as
        adults, and a memorized scripture becomes
        part of us as we worship the Lord. A simple,
        one-verse, Christ-oriented scripture can be
        learned by the whole family, at least all those
        age eight and over, in a matter of a few min-
        utes. Select one each Sunday. Learn it to-
        gether. Keep a list on the family bulletin
        board. Go back and review previous ones to
        hold them in memory.

    b. *Morning Bible Reading.* Even church-going
        families find that there is something special
        and *personal* about reading scriptures to-
        gether at home. Try gathering together fairly
        early on Sunday morning, before anyone goes
        anywhere, and reading aloud together from
        the Bible. Read slowly, with frequent pauses
        for discussion. Let children read. Try to make
        the scriptures come alive by imaging that you
        were there, in the Biblical setting, or by apply-
        ing what they say to current events and to
        today's world.

c. *Scripture goal for the week.* Try using Sunday as the day to decide as a family what will be read individually during the week. Set a goal of a few chapters (not too many) and then use Sundays as the day to catch up or finish reading the past week's assignment and to get a good start on the one for the next week.

d. *Take the scriptures to church.* Look up the references mentioned in lessons and talks; read a special verse on Christ while waiting for the sacrament meeting to start; look up questions or references as they occur to you; make marginal notes; share new-found scriptures or scriptural ideas with other family members after church.

4. *Fasting.* The principle of fasting is a more important and integral part of worship than most of us realize. In the scriptures, the word *fasting* is sometimes used as a synonym for *joy* or for *rejoicing.* Fasting can bring great peace, great rest, great renewal. Like the Sabbath, fasting was made for man and not man for the fast.

a. *Family fasting focus.* Decide, in advance of fast Sunday, on a particular need to fast and pray for together as a family. Discuss the need often during your fast and pray about it several times during the day.

b. *Family testimony meetings.* Hold a family testimony meeting every fast day. Even very small children can learn the essence of a testimony (what they believe, what they're thankful for, whom they love) and bear one of their own. Everyone in the family should be encouraged to participate, and the testimonies

should immediately precede the prayer to end the fast. They should center on Christ.

c.   *Children and the fast.* We generally under-estimate our children and their capacities. From the age of five or so, most normally healthy children are capable of missing one meal, feeling a little discomfort of hunger, and connecting that feeling to gratitude and to the giving of some of their substance to the poor who feel hunger all the time. In our family we have sponsored a third-world child through a Christian children's fund and have her picture in our home. On Sundays when we fast, the children miss a meal and know a little of how that child feels, and they under-stand that the money we save by not eating goes to help feed hungry people.

Often, by the time a child is eight or nine years old, he is capable of a full (two meals missed) fast. Again, a clear understanding of the purposes of fasting (humility, gratitude) and of fast offering (sharing, helping) are es-sential to a child's fast.

Naturally, the child should be taught to fast by example and by gentle persuasion. He should never be compelled or in any way coerced in this essentially spiritual principle.

d.   *The "perfect list."* Several years ago, one of the scriptures that we memorized as a family on Sunday was Matthew 5:48, "Be ye there-fore perfect. . . ." The children were curious about how we could be perfect at anything. So we made up a family "perfection list" on

which we decided to list any individual commandments that we thought our family could obey perfectly. The first listing was "tithing," because we felt that all of us, including the children, were keeping accurate records and pay a percentage to our church. The second listing turned out to be "fasting," because those over eight felt they could fast two meals completely. Children take a certain amount of appropriate pride in feeling that they have mastered certain of the Lord's commandments. (Caution is needed, of course, to teach children that it is the humility and gratitude felt and expressed that is the true purpose of fasting.)

e. *Partial fasts each week.* We try to fast for two meals one Sunday each month, but we sometimes have "partial fasts" (missing one meal) on other Sundays. Some families on a late church schedule find that not eating until a late morning or early afternoon brunch lends a certain humility to a family and simplifies the food preparation for the day. (This is not wise, of course, with small children who need a certain blood-sugar level to feel the peace of the Sabbath.)

5. *Prayer.* Some "special editions" of your normal daily individual and family prayers can add to the worship of the Sabbath.

a. *"Ask for" and "thankful for" item each week.* At a set, early hour, group together and discuss briefly the week past and the week ahead, the blessings received to be thankful for, and

the needs ahead to be asked for. Families with small children should pick out a particular "thankful for" and a particular "ask for" and have a child draw a picture of them. The pictures can go up by the table or wherever family prayers are held to remind the small ones of the special and unique thoughts to include in their prayers that week.

b. *Prayer before leaving for church.* Before leaving home for church, have a special family prayer about gratitude for the Atonement and the sacrament and about honoring and acknowledging the Lord in all things.

c. *Family meeting prayer.* Kneel together in your home and have a "family meeting prayer" with the Lord. Have every family member participate within the same prayer. Have one person start the prayer with "Our Heavenly Father," and say what he wishes; then when he pauses, a second family member starts, and so on until all have spoken to the Lord. The last person to speak closes the prayer "in the name of Jesus Christ, Amen." Before the prayer is closed, there should be a silent pause to give an opportunity to anyone who has thought of something additional that he wishes to say.

d. *Gratitude and acknowledgment prayer.* Try to pray individually, for ten consecutive minutes, doing nothing but thanking God for your blessings. See how many blessings you can think of. Extend the prayer to fifteen or twenty minutes if you need to.

e. *Prayer notes.* As a young missionary, I had an instructive and very memorable prayer experience with a Church leader. He was supervising our mission's activities and lived for a time in the same building where my companion and I stayed. One night, as we were ready to retire, we heard a knock at the door and opened it to find the Church leader. "May I have prayers with you this evening?" he asked. We invited him in and I invited him to pray. "No thanks," he said, "you go ahead." In his presence I tried to give an appropriately long and sincere prayer. But midway through it I heard the unmistakable sound of a pencil writing on paper. Not daring to open my eyes and look up, I assumed it was my young companion and wondered what on earth he was writing and whether he might not know who our important visitor was. I even imagined that maybe he was bored with my lengthy prayer and had decided to use the time to start a letter to his girl friend.

When I finally finished the prayer and looked up, I saw that it was not my companion but the Church leader who had been writing. A new series of thoughts rushed through my mind. *Was he evaluating my prayer? Was he bored with it?* I didn't dare ask, but he caught my eye and answered the question he saw. He answered very simply in a matter-of-fact voice, and then left, leaving me pondering his answer for most of the night, and realizing that I had not before understood what prayer really was. What he said was this: "The Lord often

gives me answers during prayer but my memory is short, so I often take notes on what he tells me."

Few of us would sit through an interview with a great man without taking notes on what he told us. Real prayer is a dialogue, and the impressions and messages the Spirit sends should be remembered and treasured.

During your special Sunday prayers, take notes. Make notes of what you ask for and of what you feel. Record the direction and message of any inspiration or answers that come to you. Have a special notebook for this purpose, or do it in your journal. Make Sunday prayer a regular interview with the Lord.

6.   *Rest.* The Sabbath admonition to rest is repeated over and over in scripture. But it does not mean rest in the sense of doing nothing.

   a.   *Rest from the world.* Try to neither think nor do anything on Sunday that is purely of the world. Rest from television, from worldly music, from sports activity (as participant or spectator), from concerns about work or finances, from school, from everything unconnected to God and to his day.

   b.   *Rest by casting your burdens on him.* The kind of rest the scriptures advocate is rest in the Lord, where we cast our burdens on him and trust in his power. The way to discontinue worry about things of the world on Sunday is to have personal prayer where you turn these worries over to the Lord and pledge to think,

during the day, about him rather than about them.

c. *Rest by meditation.* There are many current trends relating to yoga, transcendental meditation, and other kinds of techniques for shifting the brain to alpha waves and thus renewing and refreshing the consciousness. The principles and objectives are admirable, although the elaborate techniques are largely unnecessary. What is necessary is a good, sincere prayer followed by quiet moments of peaceful meditation.

There are two broad types of meditation, both of which are useful and appropriate on Sunday. The first could be called "thought" and the second "non-thought." "Thought" consists of focusing your mind on a particular scripture, the week ahead, or on some particular concern or challenge, and calmly trying to mentally organize it and sort it out. "Non-thought" is a relaxation response where one focuses his entire mind on one object or one sound (e.g., his own breathing, his own heartbeat) and shuts out all other thought, letting the mind rest and relax.

7. *Grasping the meaning of the Atonement.* It can be argued that the center of the Sabbath's worship is the sacrament and the center of the sacrament is the Atonement. Sundays then, must be a time for both ourselves and our children to deepen our testimony and understanding of the Atonement.

a. *Family classroom.* Have a place in your home

that you can use as a classroom. Have a black-board and a seating arrangement that sug-gests serious learning. Take some moments on Sunday to teach your children what you know and understand about the Atonement. Testify to them, discuss with them, simplify for them. Ask yourself what gives you your own most important insights concerning the Atonement and teach that to your children.

b. *Special books.* Small children have a very dif-ficult time grasping the idea of the Savior's ransom or atonement unless it is somehow simplified or symbolized for them. The finest example of this symbolism I have seen in all of children's literature is *The Narnia Chronicles* by C. S. Lewis. Each of these books, particu-larly the first one in the series (*The Lion, the Witch and the Wardrobe*), teaches children about the laws of justice and of mercy and helps them understand how our mistakes can be overcome only by the sacrifice of one so much greater and more perfect than our-selves. There is special significance in the final chapter when Aslan the great lion (the Christ figure) returns to life after having sac-rificed himself.

8. *Service.* We know that one of the most beautiful ways to worship Christ is to serve him, and we know that we serve him by serving our fellowman. Each Sunday, as a family, come up with one anonymous service that you can render for some-one, one secret good deed you can do together. Let a child write it down or draw a picture of the good deed so you can put it on your bulletin board or calendar for the week ahead.

Intermission

Most good stage shows have an intermission which happens just as the plot is beginning to thicken. It gives the audience time to catch its breath, to think about the first act, and to get comfortable for the conclusion.

The "plot" is beginning to thicken in this book. We've just started with the method list for Sundays, and you may already be out of breath. You may be thinking, *slow down — I barely have time to get the family ready for church, get some food on the table, and keep a step ahead of the normal day-to-day schedule — and now this book is suggesting method after method as though there were fifty free hours in every Sabbath.*

So it may be time for a brief intermission, and for a word or two of explanation and encouragement to make you more comfortable before we move into the second act and more Sunday methods.

Sundays *are* busy. They tend to engulf us in meetings, obligations, commitments, and in preparation. But the whole purpose of this little book is to try to give us the upper hand — to take us off the defense and put us on the offense — to let us act rather than react to the pressures of the day — and to make the Sabbath work for us rather than us working for the Sabbath.

There are at least sixteen waking hours on every Sabbath, and even with travel and administrative time, Church meetings usually don't consume more than a third of those hours. The purpose of this book is to help us program the precious two-thirds, the ten hours or so that remain, in such a way that we are refreshed, rejuvenated, renewed, and ready for the week ahead. And it is possible. The Lord does not give us commandments that we cannot keep. It is possible but it is not easy. It

takes a clear plan, it takes practice, it takes patience, it takes preparation on Saturday.

But the rewards are magnificent. Go back to the beginning of chapter 1 to refresh your memory.

The Sabbath can truly be the key to the rest of the week. But it is not this book, not any number of ideas, no matter how good they are, not even the power of the commandment itself, that makes the Sabbath work for us. It is you and the effort you are willing to put forth.

There are far more methods listed here than any single individual or family can use. But if you will select and choose; if you will set personal objectives for worship, for "becoming" within yourself and "becoming" within your family; and if you will *design* your own Sundays to reach toward those goals, . . . then the secret of the Sabbath's power will begin to work for you.

I suggest you write in the margins of this book. Mark the methods that you think you would like to try. Make notes on the ideas that come to you that might be even more appropriate and useful to your family than the ones listed.

Then, when you are finished reading, sit down with a clean piece of paper and write down your own goals for worshipping and for "becoming" on Sundays. Block out a schedule and include the methods you like. Work out what you will have to do on Saturday to open up the time a little on Sunday.

Husbands and wives will have to work on it together, prioritizing each other first and working around Church callings for this purpose — sharing the responsibilities so that each has individual, private time to plan and meditate and pray.

Well, the lights are blinking. Intermission is over. Let's go back into the methods, . . . perhaps with a little

more confidence that we will be able to pick and choose and *use* the activities and programs that will work best for us.

As you do, Sundays will become the intermissions of your life, the times when you pause between the one-week acts of your own drama. And the intermissions will be more than rests, for there is no set script for this drama, and you must decide on the words and actions while the curtain is closed each Sunday.

Chapter 5

The Methods *(continued)*

A. *For "Becoming" Within Yourself*

1. *Sunday sessions.* As we have discussed, Sunday can be the day in which we "sharpen our saw" so that it will cut cleanly and effectively throughout the week. But it is also a question of knowing just what we want to cut, just what our specific goals and plans should be for the week ahead. Properly used, each Sabbath can be a step on a carefully crafted staircase leading to the fulfillment of our potential and the securing of our eternal life. A Sunday session is a special block of time, spent individually each Sunday, wherein one seeks guidance, reviews his objectives, resets his course.

a. *Your own Sunday session.* Each Sunday,
preferably early in the morning, retire to a
private place, have a personal prayer about
the directions of your life, review your five-
year goals, your one-year goals, and your one-
month goals. Then set your personal objectives for the week ahead.

Many people have already adopted some sort
of system for setting long and short range
goals but the process is at its best when we
do certain things on Sunday:

(1) Start with your own knowledge of your
gifts, your situation, and your life's purpose.

(2) Develop five-year goals in the important
categories of your life—family, career, ed-
ucation, personal development, service,
etc. Five-year goals are manageable and
foreseeable; longer ones often are not. In
fact, two- and three-year goals are better
in some situations.

(3) Each new year, work one-year goals out of
the five-year goals. What must you do
this year to be on course for each of the
five-year objectives?

(4) On the first Sunday of each month develop one-month goals to coincide with
each one-year objective.

(5) Each Sunday carve out one-week goals
that take you a week closer to each one-
month goal.

Thus, the pattern each Sunday is to review the

five-year, the one-year, and the one-month goals and then to look at the week immediately ahead and set goals and time schedules for that period of time.

To those who have not tried it, the process sounds like a great chore. In fact, it is just the opposite. It is a natural and, once you are into it, an easy process that frees one's mind from anxiety during the week ahead. It allows one to act rather than react and to control many of his circumstances rather than being controlled by them.

It's nice to have a special place and time where the Sunday session occurs. I use an hourglass for concentration and timing and spend a full, focused hour. It may well be the very closest we get all week to the literal observance of the powerful admonition, "Work out your own salvation."

b. *Your spouse's Sunday session and your "couple session."* Attempt to have your individual sessions in the early morning hours. Then, later in the day, probably after the children are in bed, sit down together and share your objectives, coordinate your schedules, and work together on some of the family planning ideas suggested in the next section.

It is important for husband and wife to think and plan and pray together, but it is also important for them to do so separately. They are, as Gibran says, in *The Prophet*, individual lute strings, each with their own sound and vibration, but always in harmony, always part

of the same instrument. When planning and goal-setting starts together, one of the two usually dominates and the individual needs, gifts, and sensitivities of the other may not get full attention. But if the process starts separately and then comes together, the full range of both sets of strengths can be effectively combined.

c. *Your children's Sunday sessions.* Children, even when very small, can be effective goal-setters, and they can derive great joy as well as important training for their future from setting simple goals each week and having their days planned to reach those goals.

We have found that a simple weekly calendar form is helpful for all family members, from parents down to three- or four-year-olds. The form is essentially a seven-day calendar with two boxes above for weekly goals.

Name _____			Week _____			
S	M	T	W	Th	F	S

Each child sets two goals for the week and writes (or draws in the case of small children) them in the two boxes. The goals may have to do with music lessons or school or various kinds of self-improvement. Children should understand the difference between goals and plans (e.g., if the goal is to master a particular piece on the piano, then the plan would be to practice for a half hour each day). The goal goes in the box, and the plan goes on the calendar by virtue of lines drawn from the goal to each day when the goal will be worked on, as follows:

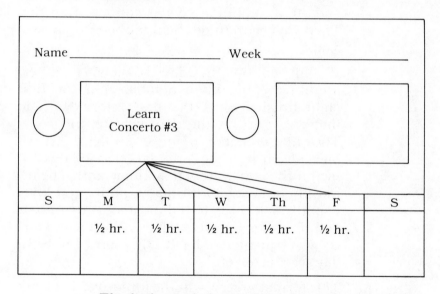

The little circle by each goal is to be colored in progressively as the goal is reached (e.g., after two days of practice, if the child felt he had progressed well, his circle would look like

this: ◕). Both children and adults find

a certain satisfaction in filling in a goal circle. It means success and accomplishment.

d. *Sunday-session-based interviews.* For several years, I tried to interview my children on a regular basis. The interviews were most often one-sided and not very effective. I would say, "How is it going, son?" He would say, "Fine." I would say, "Well, how's school?" He would say, "Fine." I would say, "Well, be more expressive; how do you feel about yourself?" He would say, "Fine."

The interviews were surface and artificial, and all of the initiative was coming from me. Then we began to tie them to the Sunday sessions.

We all do our Sunday sessions together, around the big kitchen table, and the first child finished gets the first interview. The interviews are in the den, private and cozy. The children come in one at a time; the small ones sit on my knee, the larger ones next to me on the couch (touch is important). The atmosphere is one of intimacy, pride, and love. I simply ask them to tell me about their goals and plans for the week ahead. We also review the week just passed, with their previous Sunday session sheet.

This format gives them the initiative. They are in charge. I am the listener. And their goals seem to be the perfect springboard for them to tell me their concerns and to get to what is really on their minds. Saydi might say, "My goal is to make a new friend at school." With a

little encouragement and obvious interest from me, she might go on, "because last week my friend Judy and I didn't get along." Before long the goals lead to the feelings, which is what you want to talk about in an interview. "That made me feel lonely and like nobody liked me very much." With some head nodding and some understanding looks, Saydi may think of her own solutions. "Hey, dad, maybe Judy felt the same way. Maybe my goal should be to be extra nice to her and get her back as my good friend."

The point is that when it is their goals you are talking about, it is their interview, and you become the listener-consultant rather than the talker-manager.

In this interview setting of closeness and trust, a parent can do several additional things to help a child in his own process of "becoming." During one interview my six-year-old Josh seemed a little down on himself and a little discouraged, so I started telling him some of the things I thought he was particularly good at. I told him (sincerely) that he was very good at mathematics, that he was very good at helping me fix things, that he was a very fast runner for his age. I noticed that his little face was getting brighter each minute. He was like a little sponge, soaking up the praise, needing every word of it. He liked what I was saying so much that he interrupted, "Write this down, dad, write these good things down." I said, "Okay, Josh, where should I write them?" Josh looked around, then thrust out his hand

and said, "Right here, dad, write them on my hand!" He wanted those gifts to be known. He wanted to know them, he wanted me to know them, he wanted other people to know them.

I wrote something he was good at on each of his fingers. He didn't wash his hands all day.

The next Sunday interview, he wanted to do it again. I simplified by just putting the first initial of a "gift" on each finger. That suited him just fine. The next week, I had him tell me his gifts. He did, then thought of two or three additional ones, things he really was uniquely good at.

The other kids wanted equal treatment. They all emerge from our interviews now with tiny abbreviations on the tips of their fingers. But they also emerge a little more secure in who they are, in what they can become, and in the knowledge of their father's individual and unique love for them.

2. "*Self-programming.*" The type of Sunday sessions just described orient themselves primarily to the programming of time and thus to the pursuit of external goals—things you wish to accomplish. The other kind of goals we should concern ourselves with on Sunday is internal goals—the changing of who and what we are. This type of goal requires not so much the programming of time, but the programming of self.

    a. *The "B. F. program."* Benjamin Franklin worked diligently to change and improve his personal character by selecting particular traits that he wished to have and focusing on

them, one at a time, until they were part of him. We can do the same, and we can use Sundays as our planning time. Make a list (carefully — think about it over a period of time) of the spiritual, emotional, and mental qualities you want to have. Carefully define each one, in personal terms and in writing. Put the list in your journal or your Sunday session folder. Then, each Sunday, review it. Mentally rank yourself in terms of how well you have done on each particular quality during the past week. Pick out the qualities on which you feel you need the greatest concentration during the coming week. Think ahead and try to pinpoint certain moments or occasions in the week ahead where you will have opportunity to exhibit or use those qualities.

b. *Self-description.* A variation on the B. F. program is to write a future description of yourself. Describe the person you hope to be five years from now. Write about your attitudes, your personality, your character. Be as descriptive as you can. Use examples and illustrations.

Then read the description on Sundays and monitor your steady progress toward it.

c. *Spouse description.* For some people, a description of the "future you" written by a spouse is more effective than one written by yourself.

Do one for each other. Write a description of your husband or wife five years from now. Magnify all of the good qualities you already

see. Add the other good qualities you see developing. Don't carry it so far that it becomes discouraging to your spouse, but do carry it far enough that it motivates and inspires, and causes each of you to reach for the best that is within you.

3. *Journals.* Journals are a wonderful record for posterity, but they can also be a valuable tool for self-evaluation and self-improvement.

    a. *Write your diary in advance.* Make a journal entry every Sunday. After recording your record and impressions of the week just passed, put aside your pen and, in pencil, write about the week ahead as though it had already happened. Write about the things you accomplish, the relationships you improve, etc.

        Then go out and live the week in a way that won't cause you to have to erase anything next Sunday.

    b. *Ancestor stories.* We have a wonderful, old leather-bound "minute book" which we call our "ancestor book" and in which we write, in children's story language, incidents from the journals of our ancestors. There is *Grandpa Dan and the Cat,* and *How the Eyre Name Came to America,* and *The Mountain-Moving Family.*

        The children love to hear these true stories and to point to the picture of the particular ancestor on the big family tree diagram that we have in the family room. Most of the stories are about a quality or gift of an ancestor—

their courage, their honesty, their ability as a carpenter, etc. The children identify with these qualities because they understand that a part of them came from these grandpas and grandmas. Knowing who they came from helps them in what they are becoming. We have let the children illustrate the stories in the book. Although they request it more often, we read to the children from the ancestor book only on Sundays.

c. *Small children's picture journals.* Don't wait until children can write well to start them in their first journals. If you do, some beautiful impressions and recollections will never be recorded.

Get them a good journal as soon as they are old enough to understand the concept of re-membering and recording (four or five years old). Have them draw their experiences and observations. Then label them with a few words so the drawings can be interpreted ac-curately in future years.

4. *Relationships.* Family is more important than career. People are more important than things. Relationships are more important than achieve-ments.

Yet most of us have more clear and more specific goals for the career/things/achievement aspects of our lives than we do for the family/people/re-lationships side.

Part of the reason for this juxtapositioning is that such a high percentage of our time each work day

(week day) is, by necessity, devoted to work . . . to things.

The Sabbath Day can be the time to shift this balance, to refocus ourselves on the relationship side of things. It can be the day when we think in a different way about a very different *kind* of goals . . . "*relationship goals*" rather than "achievement goals."

It is achievement goals that are most familiar to us: Reach a certain position, earn a certain amount of money, obtain a certain type of car, reach a certain sales quota, produce a certain number of something, etc. Achievement goals lend themselves to quantitative measurement, to step-by-step fulfillment, and to long-range goals that can be broken down into shorter-range goals and plans. "Relationship goals" on the other hand seem a little more vague, especially when we first focus on the concept. Let's say, for example, that someone set a ten-year goal to have a perfect relationship with his wife. What would his one year goal be? to have a 10 percent perfect relationship with her? Relationships don't quite quantify like that.

But clear relationship goals *can* be set. After all, a goal is a clear picture of something the way you want it to be at some future time. With a relationship that "future picture" has to be a qualitative description.

Here is the challenge: In a private place—perhaps at the back of your journal, write a two or three paragraph description of an important relationship as you *want it to be* in five years. Explain

and describe the relationships you want with your spouse, with your child, with your best friend, etc. Start out by writing, "It is _____ (five years from now) and then just lay out the elements of the relationship you *want*. Don't be shy or self- conscious. No one is going to read this but you. And don't be afraid of describing a seemingly *unrealistic* relationship. After all, working toward an ideal, in any type of goal setting, is how we make progress.

Write a "five-year out" description of each of your life's most important relationships.

On Sundays, take out your descriptions and read through them, sometimes adding to or refining.

Before long you will find yourself saying and doing things (without conscious effort) that move you closer to the relationship goals you have described!

C. *For "Becoming" Within Your Family*

1. *"Roots and branches."* We are told in our scriptures about the importance of turning the hearts of the fathers to their children and the hearts of the children to their fathers. We are even told that the earth will be wasted at the Savior's coming if this does not occur.

   Our fathers are our roots. Our children are our branches. We are the trunks. We can turn our hearts to our children by concentrating on them in special ways on Sundays, and some of those ways can be designated to turn our children's hearts not only to us but also to our parents and our parents' parents.

   a. *Ancestor board.* As alluded to earlier, it is useful to have a chart or painting or board that shows visually the relationship of each parent to child. Ours happens to be a large painting of a tree on a canvas. Four roots go down from the trunk, each splits to two, then each splits again so there are sixteen at the bottom. Our children's pictures are in the branches, Linda's and my pictures are on the trunk, our parents (the children's grandparents) are on the first roots, our grandparents (the children's eight great-grandparents) are on the next level, and our great-grandparents (the children's sixteen great-great-grandparents) are on the last level. They are each labeled with name and with date and place of birth. On Sundays, we move the ancestor tree from its usual place in the family room to the dining room where we can talk about it as we eat our Sunday meal.

b. *Ancestor book.* In the last section the ancestor book was described. The point is that as an ancestor story is told to children, they can point to that particular person on the ancestor board and see their connection to him, thus strengthening their identity and realizing that they have inherited some of that ancestor's qualities and strengths.

c. *Genealogy work.* As children become old enough, involve them in genealogy projects and research, much of which can be planned for and reviewed on Sundays.

2. *"Institutionalize" the family.* As mentioned in the last chapter, all strong and good institutions give security and confidence, and, in many cases, direction and guidance to their members. Our families, if they are to one day become kingdoms, must become institutions. Sunday is the best family meeting day.

a. *Family laws.* All institutions have standards and rules. In good institutions these rules are self-adopted and are a source of pride and identity to members. In families of all ages clear standards are needed, and Sunday is an ideal time to review what they are and how they are working.

Children of all ages need to learn the principle of obedience to laws. If family laws are well conceived and well established, they give children an inner feeling of consistency and security and make a family more of a democracy (obedience to laws) and less of a dictatorship (obedience to persons).

We made the mistake in our family of starting with too many laws. The kids couldn't remember them all and neither could we. Over the years we have simplified them down to only five, and each is just one word: (1) Peace, (2) Order, (3) Obedience, (4) Asking, (5) Pegs.

"Pegs" refers to peg boards which each family member has, each with four big wooden pegs. One represents his daily family job, one his music practice, one the "morning things" he does before school or work, and one the "evening things" he did before bed the night before. All four pegs must be in place each day before family prayer and dinner.

Each child understands exactly what each of the five family laws means and exactly what penalty goes with each. The laws and the penalties were arrived at and voted on together. Family laws should be reviewed and discussed at a regular Sunday family meeting, which will be discussed later in this section. Each family has to develop its own set of family laws depending on its own needs and circumstances.

One further footnote on family laws. The pivotal principle of the entire gospel is repentance, through which we can escape the consequences of sin. So it should also be with family laws. If a child can sincerely apologize, make restitution, and promise not to repeat the offense, he should be able to avoid the punishment. Nothing is sweeter than to see a child truly repent to another child, to hug him,

to ask for forgiveness, and to promise not to do it again.

b. *Family traditions and monthly calendar.* A second matter to be reviewed at the Sunday family meeting is that of traditions. Again, all great institutions have them and they can be a source of true joy and anticipation for all members. Most families already have several traditions — special activities done on holidays, birthdays or other noteworthy events. Often all that is required is to define and formalize these traditions a little.

At the back of our big leather ancestor book we have a small section for each month of the year. Listed under each month are our traditions for that month (from flying kites on Jonah's birthday in April to the annual "Children for Children" charity concert in December). In the ancestor book the children have illustrated each tradition with a little drawing. On the last Sunday of each month, one child is selected to make a family calendar for the coming month to go in the kitchen on the pantry door. The calendar shows the dates of each upcoming family tradition as well as other important dates and events. Then, each Sunday during that month, the calendar is reviewed and updated in the family meeting.

c. *Family flag.* Institutions need a banner or rallying sign. They also need a subtle or symbolic way of reminding their members of their standards and goals. A family flag can accomplish this.

Each family would want to develop their own flag ideas. Ours is used here only as an illustration. It looks like this:

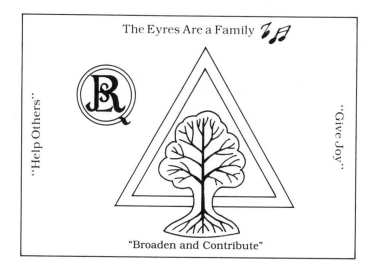

The family motto is "Help Others." The family slogan is "Give Joy." The family creed is "broaden and contribute." The family song, which we composed together, is called "The Eyres Are a Family." The triangle stands for the three things we believe are most important in life: Christ, families, and freedom. The tree stands for our roots and our branches

and our commitment to our heritage. The five corners created by the triangle and the tree stand for our five family laws. The figure inside the round ring is a collage of the first letter of all of our first names. The ring around them symbolizes eternal unity, and is also a "Q" indicating our belief that questions and being able to inquire intelligently is the basis of all learning in life. The figure also symbolizes a pupil within an eye depicting our family's belief in honesty and in looking others directly in the eye.

There are other meanings and symbolism that are not necessary to mention here. The point is that children of all ages appreciate symbolism and remember subtle representations, once they understand them, better than more direct lists. Our children, for example, remember the five family laws better from the five corners symbolized on the flag than from a written list of the laws.

The family flag should be focused on each Sunday. It should either be put away on the other six days or moved to a less prominent spot.

d. *The Sunday family meeting.* Pick a set time each Sunday and schedule the family meeting. Stick to it as consistently as the starting time for sacrament meeting or priesthood meeting. Some families may elect to do the things suggested here on Monday in connection with family home evening, but the suggestion is that these particular things are more appropriate and effective on Sunday.

The Monday family night can then be devoted to a lesson from the Family Home Evening Manual or to a family activity.

Get the family together promptly at the set time (we have a Chinese gong that gets even the little ones there in a hurry), sit in an orderly and reverent way, open with a song and a prayer, and commence.

Have an agenda that meets your own family's individual needs, but consider including the following:

(1) A review of the symbols on the family flag. Say the slogan and motto together, sing your family song, quote your family scripture, repeat your family laws; it's a little like opening a Boy Scout meeting. Take time to discuss each item as it comes up — how you are doing, where improvement is needed, etc.

(2) Look at the family calendar. Note the upcoming events or traditions, plan your week together, decide which activities require the presence of all family members.

(3) If your meeting is before church, discuss which aspect of the Savior you plan to ponder during the sacrament. (See page 22.)

(4) Decide which scriptures you will work on as a family during the week. (See pages 24 and 25.)

(5) Make assignments as to which child will prepare the "thankful for" thing, the "ask

for" item, and the "secret service." (See pages 27 and 32.)

Enjoy the Sunday family meeting. Make it a time of love and peace. Unplug or muffle the phone. Pay attention to each other. Block out the world and the concerns of the other six days and focus on each other and on eternity.

3. *Organize the family.* There is a remarkable scripture, one that is painted on a five-foot canvas in our living room, which can serve as a powerful guideline for families.

> Organize yourselves, prepare every needful thing, and establish a house, even a house of prayer, a house of fasting, a house of faith, a house of learning, a house of glory, a house of order, a house of God.

The whole verse of scripture is beautiful, but my favorite part is the first two words. If we would have our families become strong and enduring, we must organize them and organize ourselves. Organization need not be rigid or militaristic or confining. It can be creative and invigorating, and Sundays can be the pilings that support and give strength to the order and structure of a family. Sunday can be the day in which we give organization to our time, our environment, and our "personnel," and, as our family members get older, to our priesthood assignments and to the legal and financial structure of our family organizations.

a. *Time.* The Sunday sessions, family calendars, and writing our diaries in advance mentioned in earlier sections are ways to use Sundays in the organization of family time.

b. *Environment.* I stopped by a friend's house on a Saturday evening and found him and his entire family working together cleaning their house. They were really cleaning it, with enthusiasm and apparent enjoyment, and all the children, from preschoolers to adolescents, were involved. I guess my amazement showed on my face, because he invited me in for further observation and an explanation.

They all looked like teenagers with their first car — scrubbing, shining, taking pride in their work.

"We love our home," said my friend, "and we like to clean it together. On Sundays, the Lord's day, we like to think of our house as his house. We want his spirit to be with us in a special way, and we think of cleaning it on Saturday as a special invitation to him to be present here on Sunday."

Sundays can also be a time to think about simplifying your family's environment. The following idea evolved during a Sunday discussion of household organization.

We have recently decided that dressers and shelves and even beds can work against order and organization in small children's rooms. They just become collecting places for toys, unmatched socks, kitchen saucers, and the like. We now keep all small children's clothes in a large multishelved laundry room and all the toys in a well-organized playroom. The children take clothes from the laundry room and toys from the playroom one at a time, like checking out books from the library, and

return one before they take another out. Their beds are the new ones that fold, in one easy motion, into a chair.

Their rooms now have a Spartan neatness that was hitherto unimaginable. All that is in them is the chair-beds and one small chest or shelf for their very most private things. To quote my wife, "It is wonderful."

c. *Personnel.* The fine art of personnel management is a valuable skill for parents. Too often, particularly in larger families, parents run themselves ragged trying to teach all the children, feed all the children, dress all the children, etc. What is often needed is the kind of personnel organization that provides a layer of "middle management."

The day that this concept occurred to us was a real milestone in our family. Linda and I were in our Sunday "couple session" (just the two of us after the children were in bed) and were lamenting the fact that we were seriously outnumbered. There were seven of them and only two of us. It didn't seem fair. It finally occurred to us that we had to "promote" the two older children, those who were over eight, to the status of adults, to get them on our side and make the odds more even (4 to 5 instead of 2 to 7). The next Sunday we held a special meeting with them, "promoted" them with praise and appreciation, and started the practice of Sunday "adult meetings" with the older children after the younger ones were asleep. We talk about the week ahead and make assignments regarding the younger children. We decide which "joy" we want to try to teach

the younger ones that week. We decide which of us "adults" will be responsible for which parts of the house and which children's bedtimes for the week ahead. We decide who will teach the family home evening the next night. Each "adult" has a chance to voice his concerns and make his suggestions.

The whole idea of an adult-child division among your children can simplify many family functions. We often have two separate family home evenings, one for the "adult children" and one for the "children-children." Sometimes we teach a lesson to the "adults" and then assign them to teach it to the children. There are many things that can be far better taught to little ones by their older brothers and sisters than by their parents.

It is also good family personnel management to assign certain children to be in charge of certain family laws and certain family traditions. If you have a certain child who is particularly orderly by nature, assign him to be in charge of reminding other family members to be orderly. We have, among our children, "the orderkeeper," "the peacemaker," "the policeman" (in charge of obedience). We also have some of the family traditions assigned to particular children.

The point is that, especially in larger families, there is more to do and more to think about than the parents can handle on their own. Delegation is the only answer. When it is done properly, delegation compliments and recognizes children and makes their lives happier

and fuller at the same time that it makes your life easier.

d. *Constitutions and "partnerships."* As children get older, it makes sense to begin to put into document-style writing the standards, expectations, mutual relationships, and bylaws that the family wishes to adopt and live by. Things like support of each other, avoidance of criticism of each other to others, and the pledge to care for family property can all be put into a family constitution.

One aspect of a family is collective property. As families grow and children marry and leave home, efforts may be made to secure some land for common ownership, perhaps a place to hold family reunions or to build jointly-owned vacation or summer facilities. Owning property together can keep families together. Bylaws should be drawn that prevent a family member from "pulling out" or selling or mortgaging his portion.

Early in our family we set up a legal entity called a family partnership (technically a limited partnership with the children as limited partners). Over the years this partnership has earned and invested money and now serves as a sort-of family bank from which the children can borrow interest-free money to afford college.

Ideas like this can be discussed and planned for in the Sunday "adult meeting" as children reach maturity.

e. *Institutions.* As a final point in this section, it is well to remember that as we pull our fami-

lies together on Sundays, the meetings we are holding are the meetings of the most important and most basic *institutions* on earth. Important as our church meetings are, these family meetings could be more important, because families are the key building block of society. Churches can often be the support and guide to help us realize that goal. The Church is the means, but the family is the end.

Chapter 6

The Joy

A builder pauses to plan, a carpenter puts aside the board and sharpens his saw, the earth undergoes the dormancy of winter and reemerges with the freshness of spring. The very God of Heaven and Earth created and then rested.

God invites us to be the creators of our own lives and the designers of our own destinies. He gives us a special day each week on which we may do this, and he promises us not only results and progress, but also delight and joy.

He tells us to call the Sabbath a *delight.* (See Isaiah 58:13.) He uses "perfect fasting" as a synonym for "full joy," and he even tells us to prepare our food with joy on the Sabbath.

There is deep joy in working to make our lives conform to his will. There is genuine delight in feeling that we con-

trol, with his help, our own lives, priorities, and destinies. There is deep and abiding pleasure in feeling the calm, sure peace of the Holy Ghost in the inspiration that comes as we struggle in the mental and spiritual process of working out our own salvation.

One level of joy comes as we use Sundays to put our minds and our lives in order. As we plan and think ahead we take hold of our lives and gain a kind of control that brings with it joy.

But the higher level of joy comes when we learn to use Sundays to pursue our potentials, to look for God's goals for us, to give to the Lord the one thing we are sure he will never take from us—our will, as we submit to his will. The true joy of the Sabbath comes when we use that day to transmit to him our efforts to serve and to *receive* his guidance and direction.

Ezra Taft Benson said it beautifully: "Men and women who turn their lives over to God will find that He can make a lot more out of them than they can. He will deepen their joys, expand their vision, quicken their minds, strengthen their muscles, lift their spirits, multiply their blessings, increase their opportunities, comfort their souls, raise up friends and pour out peace."

Sunday after Sunday after Sunday is the time to engage in the thinking and the prayer that is necessary to turn our lives over to God and receive the promised blessings.

The purpose of mortality is the pursuit of joy. God gives to us a remarkable gift, something of his own, which contains the secret of unlocking much of this joy. Most of us never unwrap it, never understand its workings or its power. Still fewer use it regularly.

The gift . . . and the secret . . . and the joy . . . is the Sabbath.

About the Author

Richard Eyre is the author or co-author of twenty-four books, including the #1 national best seller *Teaching Your Children Values.* He believes that "self-help" is, in the long run, an oxymoron and an impossibility; that it is God, not ourselves, who can help us and change us into better and happier people.

Richard lives with his wife and fellow author, Linda, in Salt Lake City and Washington, D.C.